# D-Day – The Last of the Liberators

Some of the last veterans of the Normandy landings
retrace their steps seventy years later

Robin Savage

Foreword by Max Arthur

Helion & Company Ltd

GG Books

Co-published in 2014 by:

Helion & Company Limited
26 Willow Road
Solihull
West Midlands
B91 1UE
Tel. 0121 705 3393
Fax 0121 711 4075
Email: info@helion.co.uk
Website: www.helion.co.uk
Twitter: @helionbooks
Visit our blog http://blog.helion.co.uk

and

GG Books UK
Rugby
Warwickshire
Tel. 07921 709307
Website: www.30degreessouth.co.uk

Designed and typeset by Farr out Publications, Wokingham, Berkshire
Cover designed by Euan Carter, Leicester (www.euancarter.com)
Printed by Henry Ling Ltd, Dorchester, Dorset

Photographs and text © Robin Savage 2014
Map © Helion & Company Ltd 2014

ISBN 978-1-909982-31-4

British Library Cataloguing-in-Publication Data.
A catalogue record for this book is available from the British Library.

For details of other military history titles published by Helion & Company Limited contact the above address, or visit our website: http://www.helion.co.uk.

We always welcome receiving book proposals from prospective authors.

# Contents

# Acknowledgements

I am forever grateful to the long list of people who have assisted me with this book. Their generosity has been endless and to work alongside them was an extraordinarily humbling experience.

My first thanks must go to Jon Baker, Curator Airborne Assault - The Museum of The Parachute Regiment and Airborne Forces based at the Imperial War Museum Duxford. I approached Jon with the idea in 2011 and his support and appreciation for the project was instantaneous. Since then he has been an enormous help throughout the course of putting the book together. My further thanks go to Becks Skinner and Wendy George also at the museum.

I would like to thank Andrew Whitmarsh and James Daly at the D-Day Museum in Portsmouth for their support and time spent in research for the book. I'm extremely grateful.

I'm hugely indebted to Neil Barber for overseeing all the airborne aspects of the book. Neil is the author of some of the best books on the airborne operations of the Normandy campaign – *The Day The Devils Dropped In* and *The Pegasus and Orne Bridges* (both published by Pen & Sword), and his help has been invaluable.

I am also very grateful to Stuart Robertson for sharing his wealth of knowledge on the subject with me. Stuart lives in Normandy where he runs Normandy Battle Tours and is an expert in his field.

There are many people who helped me greatly in the early stages of the project. Penny Howard Bates, daughter of Major John Howard, has been incredibly supportive and introduced me to a number of veterans; Victoria Phipps and John Phipps at the excellent D-Day Revisited went far out of their way to allow me to photograph a number of veterans accompanying them on their annual pilgrimage; Brent Greenwood arranged for me to photograph Johnny Johnson – the first veteran I photographed for this book; Frances McClory, Secretary of the 7th Battalion (LI) Parachute Regiment Reunion Association was extremely helpful in putting me in touch with veterans from the association; Martin Kerry from the Sherwood Rangers Yeomanry Association was also very generous with his assistance; Kathryn Hadley was a huge help in liaising with the Mairies and various French authorities to obtain permission to shoot. My gratitude also goes to Brian Bould, Howard Perry, Eddie Slater – National Chairman of the Normandy Veterans Association (NVA), George Batts – National Secretary of the NVA, Béatrice Boissée and Nicolas Dumont at the Memorial Pegasus Museum in Normandy and Pascaline Dagorn – curator of the Merville Battery Museum in Normandy – her enthusiasm for the project has been wonderful.

Thanks to Dick Goodwin, who took a great deal of time to introduce me to numerous veterans and I'm very grateful for his patience on the long telephone calls we had. Thanks also to Linda Varley at the Stockport NVA; Jack Woods at the Norwich NVA; Peter Thompson, Légion d'honneur at the Surrey NVA; Michael Pine-Coffin; Ralph Bennet at Tours International; Richard & Jenny Palusinski at the Wiltshire NVA.

I would also like to thank Mark Waugh, Amy Waugh and Prasanna Puwanarajah for their help with the text of the book. Without them the writing would have been a shambles.

My thanks also go to David Cooper, Jim Howick, Steve Tagg and Guido Mandozzi for their support. Their admiration for the veterans is tremendous.

In Normandy I wish to thank the following people for the generous use of their land: Sophie Miguet at the Château St. Côme; Kevin Parkinson; Gérald Mathieu; Gilles Cuche at the Château de Beaussy; Brigitte Corbin at Le Grand Bunker in Ouistreham.

Thanks to The National Museum of the Royal Navy; Capt (Retd) Gavin Glass MBE TD of the Royal Ulster Rifles Museum; the RAF Museum in Hendon; Amy Hurst at the The Royal Marines Museum; Marie-Eve Deleris at the Juno Beach Centre in Normandy; Stuart Wheeler at The Tank Museum in Bovington.

My further thanks go to Sgt. Jim Kilbride, Jessie Dickson, Veronica Bould, Colin Read, Lauren Howick, Samantha Peters, Lucy Pearce, Frank Saunders, Karen Saunders and to Ross Savage for all the lessons in things that go bang.

Special thanks to Len Elvins who, over the last thirty years, has indulged me with stories of his time in Burma.

I'd like to also thank my publishers Duncan Rogers and all at Helion & Company Ltd and Steve Crump at GG Books for their trust, enthusiasm and their commitment to the project. I'm extraordinarily grateful. Thanks also to Ann Farr for her excellent work on the design of the book and her patience with me, and to George Anderson for the superb map.

It has been a privilege to meet Max Arthur, a man whose writing I've long admired, and I'm very grateful indeed for his foreword.

I'd like to make special mention of Fred Smith, 13th Parachute Battalion, and Ted Pool, 7th Parachute Battalion, both of whom were due to appear in the book but sadly passed away before I was able to photograph them. Their absence is greatly felt. 

I'm eternally grateful to my parents for all their love and support and for bearing with me. Thank you.

There are three people who have a very special connection to this book and any success it might achieve is largely due to their part in it. Rich Savage, Gavin Dickson and Alex Wilson, all expert image makers, assisted me whilst shooting in Normandy and their advice, steadfast devotion, stoicism, sense of humour and sheer hard work have made the book what it is. It is no exaggeration to say it wouldn't have happened without them and I'm proud to call them friends.

Finally, I'd like to thank my wife, Sophie. Over the years, Sophie has made countless trips to Normandy with me and has become friends with many veterans. This is her book as much as it is mine. Thank you for everything. You and the bump are my universe.

# Foreword

D-Day, 6 June 1944, marked the beginning of the end of the Second World War in Europe. From their bridgehead in Normandy, the Allies would push through France and after eleven months of fierce fighting, bring about the defeat of Germany.

Now, with the 70th anniversary approaching, 6 June will signal the beginning of the end again; after seven decades of ceremonies, hosted by the people of France, 2014 will be the last major anniversary attended by those who fought to give them their freedom.

Private pilgrimages will continue and families will still gather on the beaches and in cemeteries to pay their respects. However as time takes its toll, fewer and fewer veterans will make the journey back to Normandy, until eventually their number will be no more; their voices never to be heard again and the stories of their incredible sacrifice and bravery consigned to history books or recalled by their surviving sons and daughters, who may tell their children of the day that dad came back and of the stories he did or did not tell.

Robin Savage's poignant photographs are a unique record of some of the men who fought so valiantly in Normandy. He has carefully researched the location where they fought and found the very house, field or barn where many of them had their life changed forever. What happened to them in Normandy and what sights they saw and what friends they lost, will be forever etched in their memory.

Robin Savage has superbly captured the indomitable spirit of these proud men and women just in time, for we will never see their like again.

Max Arthur

These portraits are my thank you to the British veterans of D-Day. They are a tribute to the immeasurable cost and sacrifice made by so many, who gave so much to allow us the lives and freedoms we enjoy today.

For my dad, with whom I never got to make our trip to Normandy.

# Introduction

*With stout hearts, and enthusiasm for the contest, let us go forward to victory.*

General Bernard Montgomery, commander of Allied ground forces in Normandy, to troops on the eve of D-Day.

## D-Day

On 6 June 1944 the largest amphibious invasion force the world had ever seen arrived off the coast of Normandy in northern France. German troops had been living amongst the French since they invaded their country and started its occupation in 1940 and now a fleet of over 5,000 ships, with support from more than 11,000 aircraft, were sending in British, Canadian and American assault forces to free France and the rest of Europe from their grip. D-Day had come.

Germany had been at war with Russia since 1941 and in the early spring of 1944 it was well known that the long-awaited Second Front had to open soon, but no one knew where. The planners of D-Day had already decided on its location but, for fear of losing the element of surprise, it was one of the most closely guarded secrets of the war. As Hitler rightly prophesied in December 1943, 'The attack will come; there's no doubt about that anymore… If they attack in the west, that attack will decide the war.' However, through a series of ingenious British deception plans, most of the German high command were convinced the Allies would make their attack at Calais, the closest part of France to Britain.

Eighty kilometres of Norman coastline had actually been chosen, stretching from Ouistreham in the east to the Cherbourg Peninsula in the west. The beaches were split up into five assault sectors: from west to east they were Utah, Omaha, Gold, Juno and Sword. The Americans would land on Utah and Omaha; the Canadians on Juno (with significant British involvement) and the British on Gold and Sword.

To protect the flanks of the invasion zone, three airborne divisions were landed by parachute and glider ahead of the seaborne forces in the early hours of D-Day. Two American divisions, the 82nd and the 101st, landed in the west. In the east the British 6th Airborne Division made its assault. It was tasked with eliminating a large gun battery, seizing vital ground and destroying or controlling routes in and out of the area. All this was achieved ahead of the seaborne forces landing on the beaches a few hours later.

The Allies landed around 150,000 men on the day itself with fewer casualties than had been expected but, nevertheless, with significant loss of life. As the fighting progressed inland, the British would face the bulk of the German units defending the bridgehead, including eight Panzer Divisions, six of which were fanatical SS formations, and it would take two and a half months of bloody fighting through the Norman Bocage before the Allies managed to break out and chase the enemy back towards Germany.

# D-Day – The Last of the Liberators

I became interested in the Second World War at an early age, watching old footage of soldiers fighting in hedgerows with great curiosity. As I matured, so did my interest and the more I learned, the more I understood about the immense sacrifice made by the generation of men and women I'd been watching on television years before. The discovery that the hedgerows in the films were those in a particular region of northern France began my fascination with D-Day and the Battle for Normandy. Years later, in December 2011, I began a personal project that would eventually culminate in this book.

D-Day – The Last of the Liberators is a collection of portraits of some of the last surviving British Normandy veterans.

It records in a unique way the stories of these remarkable individuals and their emotional but dignified return to the locations, in many cases the exact spot, which are tied to their most profound personal memories of the campaign; places where they saw action or were wounded, where they experienced miraculous chance in the field or the loss of friends in the horror of battle.

Each June some of the last remaining veterans make the journey back to visit Normandy, with the spine-tingling tranquility of its war cemeteries and memorials, there to remember those who never came home.

The subjects of D-Day – The Last of the Liberators are representatives of this extraordinary generation.

These photographs are a record of some of the final visits these brave and dignified men and women will make to the places that imprinted themselves indelibly on their lives. They are pictures that capture an individual as they are confronted by stark memories from a haunting past.

Many books on D-Day outline in detail the planning of the operation right down to its execution and the consequent fighting inland. This book is different; it focuses solely on thirty-three veterans and their unique experiences, many of them in the face of some of the most elite units in the German Army.

The book has four chapters: airborne veterans; those that landed on Sword Beach; those that landed on Juno; and those that landed on Gold. There are introductions to each chapter to give historical context and the battalions (or the equivalent) I have mentioned are units that the veterans in the book are from. There were, needless to say, countless others involved.

Most of these photographs were taken during the 68th and 69th anniversaries of the D-Day landings. The commemorations in Normandy can often be a busy period for the veterans. It is a time for private remembrance for these individuals and I was immensely moved by the gracious kindness of the veterans and their generosity with their time. Being in the company of such extraordinary people has been one of the greatest pleasures of my life and I am honoured that many of them have become friends. I treasure memories of the hours, and in some cases only minutes, spent in the company of such gentle and noble men and women and I am only too aware that the debt we owe their generation is one that can never be repaid.

But I hope that these photographs will go some way towards ensuring their bravery and sacrifice is never forgotten.

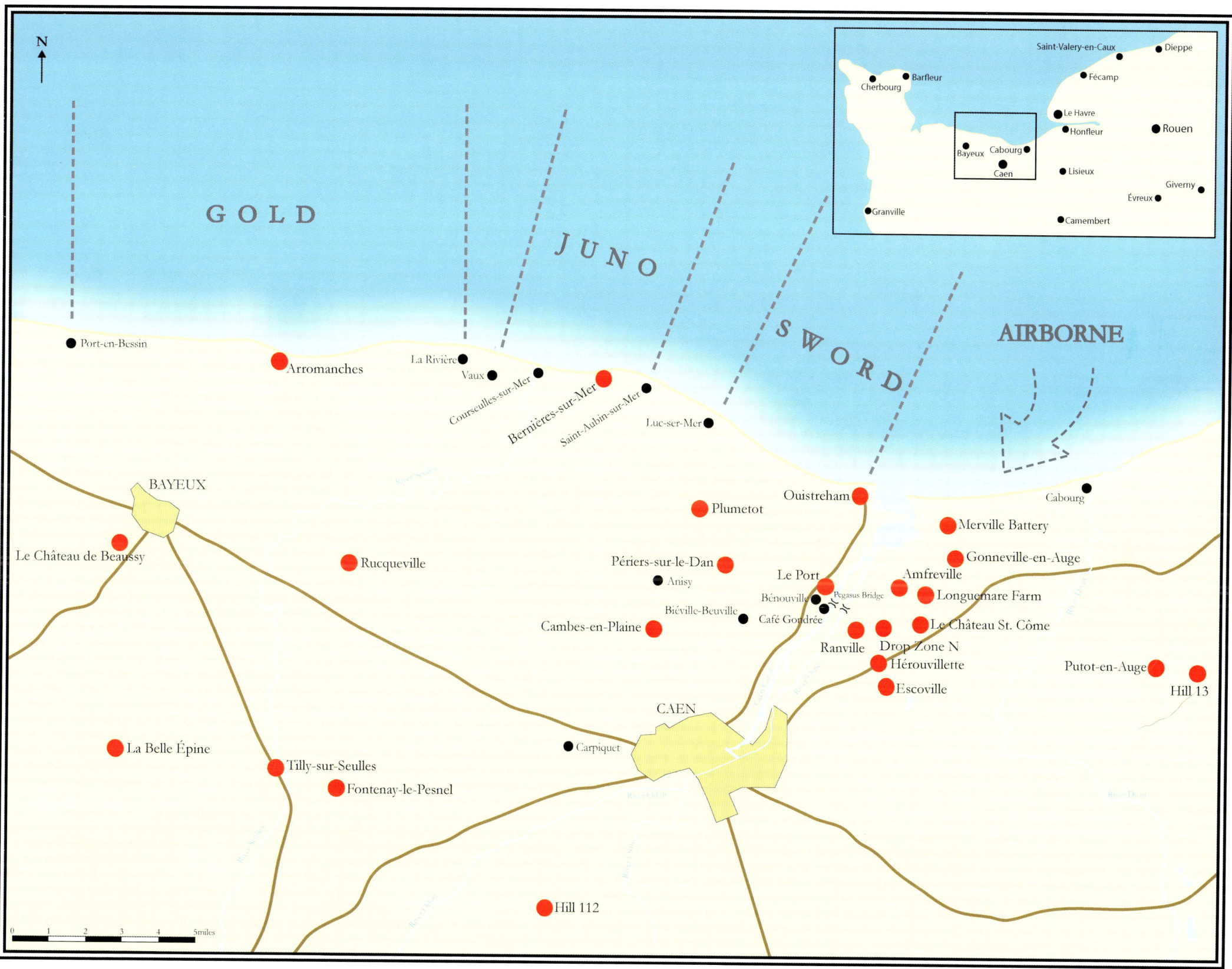

N

GOLD

JUNO

SWORD

AIRBORNE

Saint-Valery-en-Caux
Dieppe
Fécamp
Cherbourg
Barfleur
Le Havre
Honfleur
Rouen
Bayeux
Cabourg
Caen
Lisieux
Granville
Évreux
Giverny
Camembert

Port-en-Bessin
Arromanches
La Rivière
Vaux
Courseulles-sur-Mer
Bernières-sur-Mer
Saint-Aubin-sur-Mer
Luc-sur-Mer

BAYEUX

Ouistreham
Cabourg
Plumetot
Merville Battery
Le Château de Beaussy
Rucqueville
Gonneville-en-Auge
Périers-sur-le-Dan
Le Port
Amfreville
Anisy
Longuemare Farm
Bénouville
Pegasus Bridge
Biéville-Beuville
Café Gondrée
Le Château St. Côme
Cambes-en-Plaine
Ranville
Drop Zone N
Putot-en-Auge
Hérouvillette
Escoville
Hill 13

CAEN

La Belle Épine
Carpiquet
Tilly-sur-Seulles
Fontenay-le-Pesnel

Hill 112

0   1   2   3   4   5miles

AIRBORNE

Previous page:

The interior of a Douglas C-47 Dakota. Both the Americans and British used the C-47 to carry in their parachutists on D-Day. This aircraft is one of those that made the journey over to Normandy on 6 June 1944.

# Airborne

The first troops to land on D-Day were men from the British 6th Airborne Division.

In the early hours of 6 June 1944, six battalions of the Parachute Regiment and a reinforced company of the 2nd Battalion, Oxfordshire and Buckinghamshire Light Infantry, along with various other units, landed by parachute and glider to secure the eastern flank of the invasion zone.

It began just after midnight with the 2nd Ox and Bucks capturing two vital bridges over the Caen Canal and the River Orne, known today as Pegasus Bridge and Horsa Bridge. Allied control over these bridges was crucial, as firstly it would delay the Germans in bringing their armour in the east of France up to the beaches and secondly it would facilitate the reinforcement and resupply of the airborne troops to the east of the bridges. It would also provide secure access over the waterways when the Allies started to break out.

Soon after the Ox and Bucks assault on the bridges, men from the 7th and 13th Parachute Battalions from the 5th Parachute Brigade would land on Drop Zone N at Ranville. The 13th Battalion would secure and hold the village of Ranville itself. They would have the honour of being the first troops to liberate a village in France on D-Day. The 7th Battalion would head straight to the bridges to take up positions at the western end of Pegasus Bridge, around the village of Bénouville, to defend the bridgehead against inevitable German counter-attacks. Theirs would be a hard and bloody battle, but they held off everything the desperate Germans threw at them.

Meanwhile, the 9th Parachute Battalion from the 3rd Parachute Brigade had the task of assaulting and silencing the Merville Battery, a fortified site holding four artillery pieces. These guns had to be put out of action, as it was believed they could cause great damage to the troops landing on Sword Beach. Mostly due to German anti-aircraft fire and poor visibility, the 9th Battalion's drop was scattered over a large area and it took many parachutists hours, if not days, to find their way back to their units. Consequently, as the men were making their attack on the battery they were severely under strength and were missing nearly all of their heavy equipment, such as machine guns, mortars, mine detectors and plastic explosives to destroy the guns. The plan had to be re-thought on the spot.

In spite of all the problems, the assault was a success and the guns were sufficiently damaged to prevent them causing the casualties on Sword Beach the planners of D-Day had feared.

For the rest of the campaign the airborne forces faced many determined counter-attacks. Often outnumbered, they suffered daily mortar and artillery bombardments, machine gun and sniper fire and bitter hand-to-hand fighting as the resolute enemy tried desperately to break through the left flank. Despite suffering casualties in excess of 4,500 men, they held their ground.

# William Bray

## 7th Battalion, The Parachute Regiment

### Drop Zone N, Ranville

This photograph was taken on 6 June 2013 – exactly sixty-nine years to the day after William had parachuted into the fields behind him to play his part in the liberation of Nazi occupied Europe.

Unlike many others that night, William had a good drop; he landed in the correct place, unhurt and with company. Other parachutists were far less fortunate. Many were scattered far and wide from their drop zones, several were injured upon landing and some even lost their lives as they drowned after landing in fields flooded by the Germans as part of their anti-invasion defences.

William also had no trouble finding his rendezvous point. On his way there, he remembers looking up and seeing tracer bullets from German anti-aircraft fire criss-crossing the night sky as more aircraft made their way into the drop zone.

Upon arrival, he found about twenty other Paras from his battalion were already there. They could hear gunfire coming from the bridges over the Caen Canal and the River Orne as the Ox and Bucks were making their daring assault, so they knew in which direction to head.

William got to the bridges without incident and was immediately ordered over to the village of Bénouville, on the west side, to take part in their defence against the expected German counter-attack. As daylight came the onslaught began and William spent the entire day embroiled in very bitter fighting, often hand-to-hand. He was eventually pulled back to the eastern side of the bridges later that night for some rest.

Four days later, the 7th Parachute Battalion had moved on to a new location near Ranville and William was ordered to dig-in. He had just finished digging his foxhole when mortar bombs began dropping on the position. Caught out in the open, he ran to his hole but someone had beaten him to it, denying him the cover he needed. A bomb burst nearby and William was wounded by pieces of shrapnel. However the wounds were minor enough to keep him in France and he continued to fight throughout the remainder of the Normandy campaign.

# Gordon Newton, Légion d'honneur

## 9th Battalion, The Parachute Regiment

### Gonneville-en-Auge

Before the 9th Parachute Battalion commenced their attack on the Merville Battery in the early hours of D-Day, three assault gliders were due to land inside the perimeter to bolster the attacking forces. All three missed the target.

Gordon was one of the troops in glider number 26, which landed just past Gonneville-en-Auge. The time it would take them to then walk to the battery would mean they would miss the attack.

He and his platoon moved off to rejoin the rest of the battalion to get to their next objective, and as he was passing through Gonneville he found his friend Fred Glover in a bomb crater. He had been wounded and was barely able to walk. He joined Gordon's group for a while but his wounds were such that he was struggling to keep up.

A decision was made by Captain Gordon-Brown, leading the men, that Fred had to be left behind. Gordon felt very strongly about helping Fred and getting him to an aid station, as he knew he would be captured if they left him. It is a moment he has never forgotten.

Gordon went on to fight throughout the whole of the campaign, though he would return to Gonneville towards the end of his time in Normandy for a very unenviable task. He was part of a small group that had to find and exhume the badly decomposed bodies of a group of parachutists who had been accidentally killed by American bombers on D-Day, in order for them to receive a proper burial in the airborne cemetery in Ranville.

Gordon is standing on the lip of a crater made by one of the thousands of bombs dropped by Lancaster bombers in the prelude to the Merville attack, close to where he stumbled across Fred on D-Day.

# Nick Archdale

## 7th Battalion, The Parachute Regiment

### Le Port

Nick was one of many of the 7th Parachute Battalion who landed wide of Drop Zone N on D-Day. He landed safely on the east bank of the River Orne at about 01:00 and immediately made his way to Pegasus Bridge.

By the time he crossed the bridge and got to Bénouville at the western end, local German troops and tanks had just started to probe forward. They had realised the bridge was in Allied hands and there would soon be a vicious counter-attack in an attempt to take it back.

Dawn arrived at about 04:00 and with it came very heavy fighting. The Germans had worked their way into parts of Le Port, the northern end of Bénouville, and were fighting desperately to get to the bridge. Nick was sent out on a fighting patrol into Le Port to bolster the defence. Leading the patrol, which included his friend Ron Perry, they were edging along the wall in the photograph heading towards the centre of the village, when they were suddenly fired upon by a German machine gun. The bullets ricocheted off the wall just inches above their heads; one struck the wall next to Nick's eye, temporarily blinding him with fragments of brick and mortar. He stumbled into a neighbouring house where an elderly lady bathed his eyes.

The fighting around Bénouville and Le Port caused the 7th Parachute Battalion many casualties. The 104 men of A Company soon lost their commanding officer, so Captain Jim Webber, the second-in-command, took charge. Captain Webber, described by Nick as a 'tremendously brave man', was wounded several times and spent the majority of the day with a bullet in his lung, but continued to carry out his duties undeterred. By early evening, A Company had been decimated and Captain Webber was eventually evacuated. Nick was left in command of the company – it had been reduced to just eleven men.

# Ron Perry

## 7th Battalion, The Parachute Regiment

### Le Port

Behind Ron in the photograph is Pegasus Bridge and the Café Gondrée. In the early hours of D-Day, after landing safely a few hundred yards up the road, Ron made his way over the bridge as part of the force relieving the Ox and Bucks, immediately occupying a German gun position by the café. The café later became an aid station for wounded airborne troops.

Not long after dawn he was sent on a patrol into Le Port led by Nick Archdale. As they advanced along the towpath that Ron is standing on, they were fired upon by Germans holding positions in nearby houses so the patrol leapt off the path into the marshy ground between them and the houses and dashed towards where the threat was coming from, returning fire on the way.

Ron was behind Nick as he led the patrol through an alleyway, clearing houses as they went. As they reached the end of the alley they were fired upon by a machine gun, the bullets narrowly missing their heads and hitting the wall behind them. They took cover and Ron made his way into a nearby house, rushing upstairs to try and establish a firing position and get a better view of the situation unfolding outside. As he entered a bedroom, he was startled to discover a young French couple lying naked in bed. His face dirty and bloodied, the inhabitants at first thought he was a German escaping the nearby fighting, then they were convinced he was a downed Allied airman until Ron managed to communicate to them that he was a British parachutist.

The Frenchman hurried downstairs and returned with a bottle in his hand. Ron briefly 'took a minute off from the war' as they toasted the Allies, then he ran back outside to join the rest of the patrol as they were beginning to dig-in in a neighbouring orchard.

# Nick Archdale and Ron Perry

## 7th Battalion, The Parachute Regiment

### Le Port

Nick and Ron jumped into Normandy together from the same aircraft not long after midnight on 6 June 1944 and almost lost their lives against this wall later that morning.

They remain firm friends today.

# Frederick Glover

## 9th Battalion, The Parachute Regiment

### Gonneville-en-Auge

Fred was part of the glider-borne troops of the 9th Parachute Battalion who were due to take part in the attack on Merville Battery on D-Day. His glider, number 27, came the closest to the target, flying right over the top of the battery. As it did so, anti-aircraft fire came up through the floor of the glider, wounding Fred in both legs.

The glider landed about 100 metres to the east and came to rest in the hedge behind Fred in the photograph. He was only able to walk a short way and as he and the rest of the platoon got on to the road bordering the field they ran straight in to a German patrol that was heading for the battery. A firefight ensued and the enemy were forced to retreat. Had Fred's platoon not been in that position, the Germans would have been able to attack the battalion from the rear and could have caused mayhem. The platoon then went off to join the rest of the battalion but Fred could not continue.

Later in the morning Gordon Newton's platoon, which had landed further along in another glider, tried to help him but his wounds were too debilitating and he had to be left behind. He was left with two wounded Germans, one of whom was badly hurt, so Fred gave him his own morphine to ease the pain. Knowing he could soon be captured, Fred smashed his Sten gun to bits so that he was unarmed. However, he forgot certain other items.

That afternoon a German patrol approached and found them. Fred was searched and his fighting knife and a Gammon Bomb (an anti-tank hand grenade filled with plastic explosives) were found. Fred had 'enhanced' his Gammon Bomb by pushing 9mm rounds into it and when the Germans saw this they became very agitated. Fred was sure they were going to kill him, but one of the wounded Germans explained that he had given him his morphine, which mollified the situation. He was taken prisoner and eventually ended up in a hospital in Paris.

With the help of the Resistance, Fred escaped from the hospital in August and after recovering from his wounds in England, went on to fight in the Ardennes and the Rhine Crossing.

# Johnny Johnson

## 2nd Battalion, Oxfordshire and Buckinghamshire Light Infantry

### Escoville

On 7 June the 2nd Ox and Bucks put in an attack on the village of Escoville in order to establish a secure perimeter on the southern edge of the airborne bridgehead. Having landed by glider on the evening of D-Day, Johnny had been in Normandy a matter of hours when the battalion moved off towards Escoville.

The assault went in from Hérouvillette, a village about a kilometre to the north. They used 'fire and move' tactics to cover ground and close in on the village, but all too soon they were to discover that the enemy was waiting for them. Troops from the 21st Panzer Division were dug-in with well-placed machine guns on the far side of the hamlet and had supporting artillery and tanks.

The Ox and Bucks came under heavy shellfire almost immediately and started to take casualties. However they pressed on and gained entry to the village, but as the barrage lifted, it signalled the approach of German infantry and soon an all-out gun battle was raging around the streets.

Snipers were also taking their toll, but there was one less for the Ox and Bucks to worry about after Johnny's section knocked one out of the bell tower of the church, seen behind him in the photograph.

No matter how hard they fought, the German firepower was overwhelming and eventually the battalion was forced to withdraw back to Hérouvillette, where they would spend the next week being shelled and mortared and engaging in skirmishes with the enemy.

Towards the end of their time there Johnny was in a foxhole when he was nudged by his sergeant and reminded that it was his turn to go on sentry duty. He got out of the trench and started to put on his waterproof cape when almost instantaneously a shot rang out and Johnny was hit in the backside.

The Ox and Bucks paid a high price for their time around these two villages. Each year, during the anniversary week in Normandy, Johnny puts time aside to visit his friends resting in Hérouvillette cemetery.

# Lance Rooke

## Defence Platoon, 6th Airborne Division Headquarters

### Ranville

Lance landed by glider on D-Day, a week after his eighteenth birthday. He had lied about his age when signing up for the army – he was just sixteen years old.

Upon landing he was immediately sent to Ranville to defend the Divisional Headquarters, situated in the Château du Heaume. The fighting around the château was fierce and the division was losing too many of its senior officers, so it was soon relocated to a quarry on the high ground above Ranville.

Lance's role was then to take part in the air defence of the area. He spent around seven weeks on high ground overlooking the Orne valley manning a 20mm Oerlikon anti-aircraft gun, close to where he is standing in the photograph.

It was a very busy time as each night, as soon as darkness fell, German bombers would appear and try to destroy Pegasus Bridge to deny its use to the British. Lance fired 'hundreds and hundreds of rounds' in its defence. His fire was so effective that it kept the aircraft high, making it extremely difficult for them to hit their target.

However, Lance remembers the real enemies up on the ridge were the mosquitoes. Every day he and the other gunners were 'eaten alive' by the hoards of midges brought on by the hot weather and the waterways and flooded fields bordering the position.

That was until one of his friends happened upon a solution; he found that the anti-gas cream issued to the troops made an excellent repellent and soon they had all smothered themselves in the stuff, the only downside being that they spent their days 'stinking to high heaven'.

Pegasus Bridge is the pale structure visible in the distance on the far left of the photo.

# Cecil Jeffcoate

## 2nd Battalion, Oxfordshire and Buckinghamshire Light Infantry

### Hérouvillette

Cecil was part of the 2nd Ox and Bucks attack on Escoville on 7 June.

As the battalion launched their assault from Hérouvillette, Cecil was ordered to remain on the road in to Escoville manning his Vickers machine gun to protect the right flank of the attack.

He could hear the battle raging to his front and left and remembers hearing bullets ping off the bell in the church tower in front of him. As the battle began to swing in the Germans' favour Cecil was expecting the enemy to appear on the road in tanks and armoured cars at any moment. His only thought was, 'This is where I get my comeuppance'.

The attack failed and the Ox and Bucks were forced to retreat under withering fire. They moved back to their positions in Hérouvillette, taking casualties on the way.

Cecil waited and waited in this position well into the night, ready to repel a counter-attack, but thankfully the enemy never came.

The view behind Cecil in the photograph is the same view he had looking down the sights of his Vickers in 1944.

33

# Ernie Stringer

## 7th Battalion, The Parachute Regiment

### Ranville

Ernie jumped in to Normandy on D-Day and landed next to Ranville church in a field that is now the British Airborne Cemetery. As soon as his feet were on the ground his attention immediately turned to the sound of a man in great pain coming from the other side of the field. He and a few others from his platoon went to investigate and found Private Thompson, who had jumped with Ernie, lying on the ground. He had hit the side of the church on his descent and was badly injured. They gathered round and helped administer his morphine, but not having medical training there was little else they could do for him.

Sometime later Ernie was part of a group moving through Ranville who were suddenly forced to stop as they had spotted a German machine gun set up at the top of the lane. It was decided that a few men would cross the lane to distract the gunner while another handful would go around the other way to attack. They dashed across the lane and the first men got over safely but Ernie was the last man to cross and, as he did so, the German opened fire and hit him in the leg. The rest of the patrol ran off to eliminate the threat and it was not until the next day that Ernie, still lying where he was shot, was found by a medic who was able to give him some first aid and help him back to an aid station. As the pair moved away, they passed the German machine gunner, slumped dead over his weapon, efficiently dealt with by the patrol the day before.

He soon found himself at the aid station set up in the Café Gondrée where he spent four days before being evacuated back to Britain.

For a long time after the war Ernie often wondered what had become of Thompson, the wounded man he had to leave at the church, fearing he had not survived. By miraculous chance, at a 7th Battalion reunion in the late seventies, he was talking to Ron Perry and was delighted to learn from him that he had indeed survived. Ron had been best man at Thompson's wedding after the war.

# Geoff Pattinson

## 9th Battalion, The Parachute Regiment

### Le Château St. Côme, Bréville-les-Monts

On 8 June the 9th Parachute Battalion moved into positions around the Château St. Côme. The château was a dominant feature on the high ground overlooking Ranville and the vital bridges over the Caen Canal and the River Orne. It was imperative that this ground remained in Allied hands and the Germans would fight hard to take it from them.

On 10 June, after two days of heavy combat where the Paras were outnumbered by three to one, Geoff was part of a patrol that was sent forward to the château to ascertain if the enemy were nearby and in what strength. They moved via the cover of nearby woods until they reached the château and its surrounding stables and began to search the area.

After finding the château clear of enemy, Geoff and Corporal Jack Watkins moved to the area around the back of the stables to investigate further. Leading the pair, Watkins suddenly froze. He turned to Geoff and whispered, 'When I say run, run.' Watkins had spotted some Germans approaching through a field who in turn had seen them. Watkins yelled 'Run!' and the pair took off as the Germans opened fire.

They ran for cover, darting back through the open-ended stable they had come from, but as they did so Geoff was hit across the back of his legs. One of the Germans had fired through the windows of the stable into the brick walls, causing bullets and bits of brick to ricochet in all directions, wounding Geoff in the process.

This angered him so much that, after getting back on his feet, his immediate reaction was to try and get on top of a haystack to see who was shooting at them to return fire and Watkins had to work hard to convince him otherwise.

They knew they had to leave. Watkins ran to the château to warn the others of the Germans' arrival, whilst Geoff sprinted as best he could around the château and into the woods beyond.

He made it to a ditch bordering the woods that was held by the Paras. One of them leapt up, grabbed Geoff and pulled him in. Safe from the fire for now, his heart pounded away as Geoff took a moment to inspect his legs and was startled to see blood spurting from his wounds.

He eventually made it back to the Paras' main position where he received medical attention at the Regimental Aid Post before being evacuated back to England.

Geoff is standing by the stables at the Château St. Côme.

# Tony Lycett

## 7th Battalion, The Parachute Regiment

### Hérouvillette

Tony is standing near the spot where he came close to losing his life in June 1944.

About a week after D–Day he was part of a small force sent to clear a position of German troops. On entering the woods he narrowly missed being hit by a burst from a German machine gun.

He wrote to me to explain what happened:

'There is only a narrow strip of woodland remaining and the stone wall surrounding it has mostly disappeared. Seventy years ago my platoon commander, Lieutenant McDonald, of Number 1 Platoon, A Company, 7th Parachute Battalion, was mortally wounded. I was close by as we advanced towards a small broken section of the wall to enter the wood and attack a detachment of Germans who were using their positions to fire on the Ranville and Hérouvillette road, a field distant. As Lt. McDonald stepped over an observation trench dug under the wall, he received a burst from a Schmeisser. Grenades were thrown and at the double we entered the wood, finally driving out the Germans after a firefight, taking some prisoners.'

After the skirmish Tony was only one of two men left from his section. He quite rightly considered himself 'lucky to have survived'.

Tony sadly passed away on 28 December 2013.

# Jim Beasant, Légion d'honneur

## 13th Battalion, The Parachute Regiment

### Putot-en-Auge

By mid-August the Allies had broken out of the bridgehead and the Germans were in full retreat. The 13th Parachute Battalion was one of the units chasing the enemy east towards the River Seine.

As they approached Hill 13, seen in the photograph behind Jim, they were ordered to attack up the slopes in order to remove the Germans in a defensive position on the other side, there to try and slow the British advance. Jim was in the leading company of the assault.

The attack went in and as the Paras advanced up the hill they came under heavy machine gun fire, causing numerous casualties including Major Tarrant, Jim's company commander.

Jim managed to reach an orchard at the top of the hill and found himself in very close-quarter combat; he was firing at Germans who were only ten metres away. Suddenly, his Sten gun jammed. He discarded it and started looking around to try and find a rifle from one of his fallen comrades when he was called over by another Para, Private Malloy. A Bren gunner had been killed so Malloy was now manning the weapon and needed Jim's help. Jim rushed over and acted as his number two, feeding Malloy a fresh magazine each time he expended one.

The pair were using the gun to great effect, until the inevitable happened; they used up the last magazine and were now out of ammunition. Malloy turned to Jim and asked, 'What are we going to do now?' but before Jim had time to reply, a German grenade came over a hedge and landed beside Malloy, killing him instantly. The blast knocked Jim out and when he came to he found that not only was he wounded and disorientated but he was also trapped. Due to the heavy German fire he was unable to get back down the hill to his own lines and was soon taken prisoner.

The Germans took Jim across the Seine to Lillebonne where he was held in a school that was being used as a hospital. But two weeks later the Canadians caught up with the German retreat, causing them to flee and leave Jim in their hands.

He was taken to a hospital in Bayeux to recover from his wounds and went on to fight with the battalion in the Ardennes and the Rhine Crossing.

41

# SWORD

Previous page:

Sword Beach at sunset. The assaulting troops from the British 3rd Division landed along this stretch of beach. On D-Day, the two large houses on the far left of the picture were part of a German defensive site codenamed *Strongpoint COD*. This was a formidable position consisting of weapons pits, machine guns and 50mm anti-tank guns and caused numerous casualties.

# Sword

Sword Beach was the easternmost of all five invasion beaches. It ranged from Ouistreham, on the edge of the estuary of the River Orne and the Caen Canal, to Luc-sur-Mer, eight kilometres to the west. Due to offshore reefs the designated landing zone was restricted to just 1,450 metres, making it wide enough for just one brigade to land at a time.

The job of assaulting the beach was given to the British 3rd Division. The division consisted of three infantry brigades: 9th Brigade, which included 2nd Battalion, The Royal Ulster Rifles, 8th Brigade and 185th Brigade. 1st Special Service Brigade, which included No. 3 Commando, also landed on Sword and was temporarily under 3rd Division's command. Armoured support came from 27th Independent Armoured Brigade.

The division's main objective was the capture of the Normandy capital, Caen. General Bernard Montgomery, commander of Allied ground forces in Normandy, considered this to be of the utmost importance, as then he'd be able to consolidate his forces, make use of the city's important road and rail junctions and then launch his troops from there on to further objectives. He planned to take Caen on D-Day itself, however it was unknown at the time of planning that the 21st Panzer Division were in close proximity to the city.

The landings were due to commence at 07:25 to coincide with those at Gold Beach. While the division was fighting its way towards Caen the commandos would secure the eastern and western flanks of the landing zone, clear the town of Ouistreham and then rapidly move five kilometres inland to cross the bridges over the Caen Canal and the River Orne to link up with the airborne forces, where they would then come under command of the 6th Airborne Division.

Due to the importance of Caen and the formidable beach defences, naval support at Sword was tremendous. At 05:50 three cruisers, nine destroyers and numerous rocket ships let loose a deafening barrage as they engaged the defences on the beach and further inland. Allied aircraft bombing the coastline added to the onslaught.

As the assault units hit the beach they initially suffered heavy casualties but, due to the fact that enough tanks arrived at the beach on time, the infantry were able to co-ordinate their attacks with them as planned and by 10:00 most of the strongpoints were overcome. By late afternoon the leading battalion from the division had reached the villages of Beuville and Biéville, only three kilometres short of Caen. Their objective was in sight. However, the battalions that were due to take the city with them had been relocated to reinforce weaknesses elsewhere within the beachhead. Now dangerously exposed and severely outnumbered, the leading battalion was stopped in its tracks by the arrival of tanks, assault guns and infantry of the 21st Panzer Division. This was the crisis they had feared; the Germans had halted the advance and they were now preparing a massive counter-attack to drive the British back into the sea.

Having failed to link up with the Canadian 3rd Division coming from the west, there existed a four kilometre gap between Juno and Sword and at 16:00 the 21st Panzer Division launched an assault right in to the middle of it. But the British were ready for them. They replied with fighter-bombers, their own tanks (including the fearsome Sherman Firefly) and self-propelled guns and within two hours the attack was over.

Meanwhile, the commandos had performed well and made contact with the 6th Airborne Division as planned. On 7 June it was believed that the Merville Battery was shelling Sword Beach, so it fell to No. 3 Commando to put in a second attack to silence it permanently. Ferocious as it was, the attack was ultimately unsuccessful.

By the end of the day the British had landed around 29,000 troops but they suffered losses of around 700 men. German casualties were much higher. The troops on Sword Beach had repelled the only serious counter-attack along the whole of the Normandy front that day, but the capture of Caen was much too ambitious for a D-Day objective. The Germans soon rushed forward the vast majority of their reserves in to this sector, including most of their SS Divisions, meaning the city would stay in enemy hands until 9 July.

# Peter Thompson, Légion d'honneur

## Royal Navy, aboard a Landing Ship, Tank

### Sword Beach

Peter joined the Navy in 1942. After six months of basic training he was sent to sea to gain experience. In late 1943 he was put on an LST (Landing Ship, Tank), a large craft designed for amphibious operations that had the ability to beach itself in order to deliver its cargo of vehicles and personnel directly on to dry land. Peter's role was to remain by the bow doors and make sure all the cargo and troops got away smoothly.

At 07:30 on D-Day, while still out at sea, Peter's LST released its load of eighteen amphibious vehicles to join the assault on Sword Beach. At 10:00 the LST landed on the beach itself to deliver the remainder of its cargo of trucks containing ammunition for the tanks.

They stayed on the beach for eight hours, waiting for the tide to rise, which would give them the ability to return to sea. They were under constant artillery and machine gun fire. Peter occasionally had to take cover but he was so busy on the ship that he 'almost didn't notice it'. Throughout the day the ship was taking wounded on board so that they could carry them to Portsmouth when they finally made the journey back. In total, they took onboard 500 casualties before returning to the water.

A few days later, on approaching the French coast to land further troops on Sword Beach, Peter heard a voice behind him say, 'I've slept with this man's mother.' He turned around and was startled to see his brother, Ray. Ray was in the Royal Army Service Corps and part of the follow-up forces landing in Normandy. They had only a few minutes together, but in that time Peter managed to load him up with fresh loaves of bread and tinned sausages to take ashore. As Ray disembarked from the ship Peter felt helpless, watching his brother move off the beach and into the battlefields of northern France.

Peter made twenty such trips from England to Normandy to bring in tanks, troops and supplies to reinforce the front line units fighting their way inland.

# James Clegg

## Royal Navy, aboard HMS *Frobisher*

### Le Grand Bunker, Ouistreham

Among the ships laying down the massive barrage on Sword Beach ahead of the assault troops on D-Day was HMS *Frobisher*. On board was Petty Officer James Clegg, then a twenty-three-year-old Electrical Artificer.

Moments before the barrage commenced James remembers Captain Mudford, the ship's captain, giving the order over the loudspeaker to 'flatten Ouistreham.' She opened up with her 7.5-inch guns and began the destruction of the Norman seaside town.

Two hours later, as the infantry arrived on the beach, the barrage lifted. Unbeknownst to her crew at the time, the *Frobisher* had scored a direct hit on a huge German bunker in the middle of the town that commanded many of the gun batteries in the area. Towering over the local houses, it had excellent views over Sword Beach and the mouth of the Orne waterways and was able to call down artillery fire at a moments notice. The *Frobisher's* shell had struck the observation room and taken the roof clean off it, knocking out the rangefinder in the process and rendering the bunker useless.

Now fully restored to how it was on 6 June 1944, James is standing in the exact room destroyed by the *Frobisher* on D-Day.

# Bert Beddows

## No. 3 Commando

### Merville Battery

The 9th Parachute Battalion's attack on the Merville Battery had silenced it for most of D-Day. However, by 7 June the Germans had recovered and it was believed the Merville guns were starting to fire on men from the follow-up forces coming ashore on Sword Beach. Another attack had to be put in.

Two troops of No. 3 Commando were given the job. Bert had already encountered sniper fire when crossing Pegasus Bridge and had taken part in fighting around Ranville, but the attack at Merville was to be like nothing he had witnessed before.

On their approach to the battery the commandos were mortared and Bert was nicked on the shoulder by a piece of shrapnel. Undeterred, he pressed on with the rest of his troop and began forming up for the assault.

They charged the battery but were instantly met with a hail of mortar and small arms fire from an enemy determined to hold on to the position. Machine guns raked the attackers and a Bren gunner beside Bert, Trooper Abrams, was hit in the arm by thirteen bullets. He was in a very bad way, so Bert grabbed Abrams' Bren gun and, leaving him in the temporary safety of a bomb crater, ran to get help. He was immediately sent back with a sergeant to find Abrams but amid the chaos of the battle they were unable to locate him.

Despite the determination of the defenders, the commandos managed to reach the casemates housing the guns, two of which are seen behind Bert in the photograph, but as they were struggling to crack open the steel doors the Germans brought up two self-propelled guns and began firing on the commandos.

Bert was selected to be part of a five man fighting patrol sent to knock out one of the self-propelled guns. They moved off and almost immediately came under sniper fire. The group took casualties and before long there was only Bert and another trooper left. Bert sprinted to a ditch to take cover from the sniper, but as the other commando made the run he was cut down by a machine gun half way across. Completely outnumbered and out of options, the Germans closed in on Bert and he had no choice but to surrender.

He was taken to Stalag IV-B in east Germany, a journey that took several weeks, and it was here that he ran into Abrams again. It saddened Bert to see that his arm had not received the proper attention it had needed and had been duly amputated, but at least he was alive.

During the winter he was part of a group of prisoners taken out of the camp and marched west to avoid the approaching Russians. They were on the road in the biting cold for around three weeks, a time that Bert describes as 'hell on earth'. There was no food, no organisation and the German guards were 'ready to pack up anyway' so, in true commando style, Bert and a friend decided to 'take over the column'. They disarmed the guards and travelled west until they ran into the advancing Americans.

# Percy Lewis

## 1st Buckinghamshire Battalion (part of 6th Beach Group), Oxfordshire and Buckinghamshire Light Infantry

### Ouistreham

The 1st Buckinghamshire Battalion's role on D-Day was to ensure stores and ammunition for the assault battalions of Sword Beach got safely ashore and were well organised. They were also responsible for the immediate defence of the area against counter-attack.

As he approached his designated landing zone on the afternoon of D-Day Percy was met by a tangled mess of burning tanks, upturned lorries and the battered bodies of men who hadn't survived the landings.

On 7 June he moved to Ouistreham into a position at the northern end of the ground between the Caen Canal and the River Orne.

He and other men from his company were told to occupy the bunker in the photograph, previously inhabited by German troops. In the immediate days that followed a telephone in the bunker would ring and ring. Percy was ordered not to answer it. It transpired to be Germans calling from a command bunker a few miles inland desperate to find out what was happening at the coast, unaware the bunker had been cleared by Allied troops on the day they landed.

By using the periscope that extended out the top of the bunker, Percy could see Germans on the banks on the far side of the mouth of the river, visible in the background of the photograph, and was able to keep watch on them. From this position Percy was well within range of sniper fire so, outside of the bunker, he had to move around with extreme caution.

He remained here until mid-July, spending his time either keeping guard in the bunker or helping unload stores from trucks landing on the beach.

In an effort to break the routine one day he and some friends gathered up a number of German stick grenades they had found earlier in the bunker and tied them into a bundle. They put them into a sack, pulled the cord on one and hurled the device into the canal. The ensuing explosion was so huge that not only did it bring up a number of dead fish (which a nearby Army cook was very grateful for), it also caused the enemy on the far river bank to believe they may be under attack and send over a salvo of shells in reply. Fortunately for Percy they were as poorly aimed as they were unwelcome and they crashed safely into the canal behind him.

# George Lines, Légion d'honneur

## Royal Signals Troop attached to Headquarters, 4th Army Group Royal Artillery

### Plumetot

George landed on Sword Beach on 9 June in a 15cwt radio truck, known by the troops as a Gin Palace.

He was immediately taken to Plumetot, a small hamlet four kilometres from the coast, where his truck was stationed in a copse. As a wireless operator, George's job was to communicate target coordinates to five regiments of artillery. He was one of three men operating the radio in the back of the truck and would work in a shift pattern, sleeping in a nearby slit trench when he had the chance.

On 18 July Montgomery launched Operation Goodwood – a huge offensive designed to capture territory on the outskirts of Caen still held by the enemy and break through the stiff German lines east of the city to exploit the open ground beyond it.

The operation was preceded by a massive artillery barrage consisting of 760 guns with 297,600 rounds of ammunition, of which 4th Army Group Royal Artillery was part. The intense shelling of pre-determined targets was so fierce that the commander of one Tiger Tank unit on the receiving end of the barrage reported that it had led to one of his men going mad and another two committing suicide.

As the operation proceeded George continued to pass on locations of targets to the regiments as the advancing tanks and infantry called them in. However, the Germans soon recovered from their initial shock and put up a firm resistance. Their network of well-constructed defensive positions and deadly 88mm guns, along with the arrival of bad weather that caused the British tanks to get bogged down, stopped the operation dead in its tracks and on 20 July Goodwood drew to a close.

George stayed in Plumetot until mid-July and continued his role within 4th Army Group Royal Artillery right through the Normandy campaign.

# John Shanahan

## 2nd Battalion, The Royal Ulster Rifles

### Cambes-en-Plaine

On 9 June the 2nd Battalion of The Royal Ulster Rifles attacked these woods in Cambes-en-Plaine to drive out determined and fearless troops from the 12th SS Panzer Division – the *Hitlerjugend*. John was in the centre of the attack.

He landed on Sword Beach on the morning of D-Day and remembers the landing being incredibly noisy. 'There were munitions running overhead like express trains. I wondered how on earth I was going to get through that'.

As part of the move towards Caen, D Company of the 2nd Battalion put in an attack on the woods on 7 June. Intelligence led them to believe the woods were lightly held, so the Ulsters had a nasty shock to discover they were defended by such an elite unit who would fight hard for every inch of ground. A fierce battle ensued, resulting in numerous casualties and the Irishmen eventually retreating.

Two days later a second attack was put in. Now aware of the enemy they were facing, the entire battalion was used for this assault with support from Sherman tanks and naval gunfire. They formed up around the village of Anisy and began their advance through open cornfields. Again there was bitter fighting. John's predominant memories are of men dropping all around him and wondering if he might be next. But this time the Ulsters were successful. They liberated Cambes and the Germans were driven back – but at a cost to the battalion of 200 men.

However, they were far from safe. Still under fire from German snipers and mortars, John stayed in Cambes for the next couple of days assisting the wounded and collecting bodies of the dead, before the battalion eventually moved out of the village and pushed on towards Caen.

# Roy Cadman

## No. 3 Commando

### Amfreville

After landing on Sword Beach at 09:05 on D-Day, No. 3 Commando crossed over Pegasus Bridge into the airborne sector to support the Paras in their operations. Roy's troop first stopped in Ranville to help the 12th Parachute Battalion before moving up to Amfreville to make contact with the 9th Parachute Battalion. They arrived in the early hours of the following morning.

At the northern end of the Bréville Ridge, Amfreville was part of the high ground that had to be held by the Allies to protect the left flank of the entire invasion zone and to deny the enemy views over the critical bridges spanning the Orne waterways.

As Roy entered the village there was already a battle raging. Another troop had gone on ahead of Roy's during the afternoon of D-Day to find that men of the 9th Parachute Battalion had been doing a gallant job of holding on to their positions around the Château d'Amfreville as they were fired upon by an enemy that heavily outnumbered them. The Paras were running desperately low on ammunition and relief from the commandos had come in the nick of time.

Amfreville was a place Roy would get to know well. His unit spent the entire campaign in the village engaging in regular battles with the enemy who were continually attempting to dislodge the commandos.

A week after D-Day the Germans put in a regimental attack. It was of such a size that the might of the 25 Pounder field guns supporting the commandos had to be brought down on the advancing enemy. The effect was devastating but still the Germans came on. The battle then took a turn for the worse with the arrival of three German tanks, but the commandos had a trick up their sleeve; RAF Typhoon fighter-bombers were called in and within minutes had reduced the tanks to burning wrecks. The commandos finally started to gain the upper hand.

As Roy surveyed the scene he saw 'German bodies all over the place.' In fact their fire was so effective that the Germans had to call for a cease-fire to collect their dead and wounded. Commando medics went out to help them with their task.

All in all, Roy spent about two and a half months in Amfreville. Shelled or mortared nearly every single day, he played his part in preventing the enemy from taking a piece of land they so desperately wanted.

Roy has been photographed in what remains of the Château d'Amfreville today.

# Fred Walker

## No. 3 Commando

### Longuemare Farm, near Amfreville.

Longuemare Farm was situated about half way between the German and the commando positions near Amfreville. A dominant feature in no-man's land, it was important to both sides as it offered views of each other's slit trenches and the chance to fire upon them.

The farm changed hands numerous times, the exchange of ownership usually being preceded by a short, sharp firefight. However, depending on the nerve of the German troops holding it at the time, the approach of a commando fighting patrol was often enough to drive them off and they would slip away without a shot being fired.

It was clear to the commandos whenever the Germans had occupied the farm. After having taken part in the second assault on Merville Battery on 7 June, Fred spent the next few days around Amfreville and remembers from his time at the farm that 'You could tell the Germans had been there. You could smell their soap'. The enemy would often exit the farm with such haste that they would occasionally leave behind half-cooked meals, which was always a welcome surprise for the commandos.

Once inside the farm they would harass the Germans as much as they could. Sniping and firing their 2-inch mortars caused the Germans to keep their heads down and prevented them from going about their daily duties, whilst giving the commandos freedom to move about in relative safety. They also had a German-Jewish interpreter with them who, having fled Germany at the outbreak of war, held a deep hatred for his homeland and would shout abuse at his fellow countrymen as they took shelter in their slit trenches.

On 12 June, whilst in Amfreville, Fred was wounded in the foot by a mortar and was evacuated back to England. The same blast killed John Tupper, a good friend of his. They had been close since taking part in the raid on Dieppe in 1942.

# Kenneth Sturdy

## Royal Navy, attached to No. 41 Royal Marine Commando for the landings

### Périers-sur-le-Dan

Kenneth joined the Navy in 1941 and spent his first three years as a Petty Officer aboard North Atlantic Royal Navy Convoy Escort Vessels. In 1944 he was transferred to Combined Operations in preparation for the Normandy landings.

He landed on Sword Beach early in the morning on D-Day. Once ashore, his task was to provide a communication link between the military combat units inland and the naval offshore fleet; where the Army needed naval guns to support their action, Kenneth, via radio, could bring about an instant response.

When Operation Goodwood opened on 18 July, Kenneth was stationed with his radio gear on high ground in Périers-sur-le-Dan, six kilometres north of Caen. As the first bombs from the RAF and USAAF, and shells from supporting artillery, rained down on enemy-held locations all around the city, the payload from one bomber fell short and straddled Kenneth's position.

As the bombs crashed down around him Kenneth dived into a nearby ditch for protection. The earth shuddered as the ear-splitting explosions went off just metres from him. Once it had lifted he was only too thankful to realise that he had escaped unscathed, although extremely shaken.

As the dust settled, Kenneth fumbled in his tunic for a cigarette to calm his nerves. He nudged the man huddled next to him in the ditch to ask for a match but, when he turned round, Kenneth was astounded to find that it was his brother, Norman. They hadn't seen each other for four years. The last time they met it was in Luton and Norman was a college student. Now here he was, crouching in a ditch in Normandy in RAF battle-dress.

It transpired that Norman had joined the RAF in 1942, had landed on Sword Beach on 9 June and was now on his way to Carpiquet Airfield to help set up the British base there once it had been seized from the enemy. He happened to be passing over the high ground and took shelter in the same ditch as Kenneth as the bombs began to fall.

The ditch now filled in, Kenneth is standing on the exact spot that his extraordinary encounter with his brother took place in 1944.

Juno Beach. This bunker was assaulted by a platoon from B Company, The Royal Winnipeg Rifles, led by Lieutenant W.A. 'Cosy' Aitken. The Canadians suffered very heavy losses and Aitken himself was badly wounded in the attack, but they took the bunker. Engineer reinforcements then toppled it with demolition charges, giving 'Cosy's Bunker' the characteristic slant it still has today.

# Juno

Juno Beach was located between the two British beaches, Sword and Gold. It stretched from the hamlet of Vaux, just east of Gold, to Saint-Aubin-sur-Mer, west of Sword. It was to be initially assaulted by two brigades of the 3rd Canadian Infantry Division, although the landings involved many British personnel too. The Canadian 8th Brigade, which included troops from the Queen's Own Rifles Of Canada and Le Régiment de la Chaudière, would land at Bernières-sur-Mer, whilst the 7th Brigade would disembark at Courseulles-sur-Mer. Royal Marine Commandos would land directly behind the assaulting troops with a final follow-up wave from the Canadian 9th Brigade. The D-Day objectives of the 3rd Canadian Division were to capture the aerodrome at Carpiquet and to reach the Caen–Bayeux road, forming a link between the two British beaches.

As per the plan, the landings on Juno commenced thirty minutes later than those on its neighbouring beaches to allow the rising tide to cover underwater rocks previously spotted by air reconnaissance (which turned out to be mostly floating seaweed), but they were delayed by a further ten minutes owing to bad weather. As the landing craft approached they came under heavy fire and many were destroyed after colliding with anti-tank mines attached to submerged obstacles. Resistance from the German 716th Infantry Division defending the sector was stiff and the 8th Brigade took heavy casualties in the opening minutes of the first wave.

Just like troops fighting their way ashore on the other beaches that morning, the Canadians were horrified to discover that a great number of the gun emplacements were actually sighted along the beach and not out to sea, making it much easier for the Germans to cut down the advancing infantry. Many men ignored the order to leave the wounded, stopping to help their fallen comrades.

Those defensive positions that were too hard to overcome quickly were left behind for the follow-up forces so that the units already on the beach could press on inland. By mid-morning, after much bitter fighting, Bernières-sur-Mer was finally in Canadian hands.

The 3rd Canadian Division landed 21,400 men on 6 June 1944. They made the greatest advance that day and got troops further inland than any other unit on D-Day, but at a cost of just under 1000 casualties.

# Ted Emmings

## Royal Navy, coxswain of a Landing Craft, Assault

## Juno Beach

Ted's landing craft was carrying a platoon of thirty-six men from The Queen's Own Rifles Of Canada and four naval crew as they approached Juno Beach on D-Day. They were part of the first wave of assault troops.

He'd been instructed to use a large house on the seafront at Bernières-sur-Mer and a bunker just to the left of it, both easily identified on his approach to the beach, as a guide for where he was to land his troops. He arrived amid a hail of gunfire, bang on target.

As he neared the beach his landing craft hit an obstacle, which detonated the mine attached to it, badly damaging the starboard bow just in front of Ted. The damage was so bad that infantry and crewmen had to kick the ramp at the front of the craft in order to lower it so the troops could get out and on to the beach. This took some time, by which point they'd attracted a considerable amount of attention from the German defenders, particularly from the bunker. Many of the troops were cut down as they left the craft. Ted remembers one of his crew getting into the sea to help the wounded but he too was shot and killed.

As his craft left the beach they hit another mine, this time in the stern, which killed the stoker. They got a little further out to sea before they finally sank. A passing landing craft picked up Ted and the surviving crew.

Ted is standing by the bunker, with battle damage still visible. The house, known today as Canada House, is on the far right of the picture. He is friends with the occupants and visits them every year on 6 June to remember those who fell that morning.

# James Baker, DSM

## 544 Assault Flotilla, Royal Marines

### Bernières-sur-Mer

James was in the second wave of troops to assault Juno Beach on D-Day. His job was to lead the troops in his landing craft – men from the French-Canadian Le Régiment de la Chaudière – in the attack.

As he neared the beach he gave a thumbs-up to his friend Corporal Walker in the neighbouring landing craft. As he did so, Walker's craft lifted on the crest of a wave and, to his horror, James saw three anti-tank mines attached to an obstacle protruding from the water under the bow of the craft. It struck the mines and the resulting explosion not only destroyed Walker's boat but caused James' to sink too.

He swam ashore with his men and as he reached the beach, sodden and afraid, his only thought was to carry out his duties and lead the Chaudières into battle. Leading from the front, he stepped over the bodies of the Canadians cut down only moments ago by the hail of enemy fire he was now facing and got them to the top of the beach.

Their numbers were rapidly depleting. James knew they had to silence a bunker that had accounted for many of the casualties on the beach. He and his sergeant made their way through the barbed wire, approached the emplacement and handled the job with brutal efficiency using the sergeant's flamethrower.

They then moved on to the town square of Bernières, less than a kilometre from the beach, and upon arrival their next job was to deal with a sniper in the church tower. Again, James and his Chaudières completed the task with similar effectiveness.

About an hour later, while standing by the church door in the photograph, James was severely wounded by a mortar from a Nebelwerfer, a six-barrelled German weapon that would strike fear into the hearts of men just by the sound it made alone.

Unconscious and on his own, it was pure chance that two medics happened to pass by soon afterwards. His tongue was blocking his airway and unable to prise his jaws apart, the medics had no choice but to take James' bayonet and smash his front teeth out in order to save his life.

James was awarded the Distinguished Service Medal for his actions on D-Day.

# Gold

Right in the middle of the Allied landing zone in Normandy lay Gold Beach. It was the most westerly of the British beaches, resting between Omaha, one of two American beaches, and Juno. It ranged from Port-en-Bessin in the west to La Rivère in the east.

Attacking the beach would be the British 50th Infantry Division. 8th Armoured Brigade, which contained three squadrons of tanks from the Nottinghamshire Yeomanry, Sherwood Rangers, had been attached to the division for armoured support. They would supply one of the many novel inventions created for the landings – Duplex Drive tanks. Known as DD tanks, these were Shermans equipped with propellers and high canvas screens enabling the tanks to float. They were to be launched several kilometres out to sea and would then swim ashore, dropping their screens on arrival at the beach giving them the element of surprise. They would immediately attack the beach defences, thus providing the first wave of troops arriving minutes after them with adequate supporting firepower.

50th Division's D-Day objectives were the capture of Bayeux and the Caen-Bayeux road to hamper German counter-attacks, and to link up with the Americans coming from Omaha and the Canadians coming from Juno. The seizure of Arromanches was also critical as this was to be the site of one of two Mulberry Harbours, huge artificial ports built days after D-Day to facilitate the reinforcement and resupply of the advancing troops.

The first infantry units to land, arriving on time at 07:25, were 231st Brigade, which included 2nd Battalion, The Devonshire Regiment, and 69th Brigade. Due to rough seas, a last minute decision was made to take the DD tanks all the way to the shore as they would otherwise most certainly flounder and sink (a point proved on Omaha where all but a few of the tanks sank without trace after they were launched at sea as planned). However, this meant that the first wave of troops fought alone without any support from tanks until they arrived at 08:00.

Further to that, the naval bombardment that had been raging since 05:50 had mixed results; in some parts, the garrisons of resistance nests were almost driven mad by the barrage and were rendered totally combat ineffective. Whereas at La Rivère, even though it came under fire from over 3,000 shells and rockets, a German 88mm gun housed in a massive concrete casemate survived intact.

For a moment there was much confusion on the beach (the commanding officer of the 2nd Devons couldn't find a single man from his battalion upon landing), but the Germans failed to take advantage of the opportunity to inflict heavy casualties and by 08:30 the British started making progress.

The follow-up brigades arrived at 11:00. 151st Brigade, including the 6th Battalion, Durham Light Infantry, and 56th Brigade provided welcome momentum to the attack and by midday the division was moving inland.

By the end of the day the troops assaulting Gold Beach had established a firm foothold and had linked up with the Canadians coming from Juno. They got within a kilometre of Bayeux and had taken Arromanches, ready for the arrival of the Mulberry Harbour. 25,000 men had made it ashore but around 1,000 men were lost in doing so. Of the German units defending the area, some had suffered very high losses; others had been completely destroyed.

# Albert Jenkins

## B Squadron, Nottinghamshire Yeomanry, Sherwood Rangers

### Gold Beach

Albert was Co-driver of a DD Sherman tank that swam ashore in the early stages of the landings. His was the first tank to land on Gold Beach on D-Day.

As the tank crawled out of the surf and on to the beach, it was immediately hit by a shell and knocked out. Albert and his crew started to bail out, but as they scrambled through the hatch in the turret they were shocked to see the flotation screen that surrounded the tank ablaze, preventing them from getting down. They were momentarily stuck in the tank and extremely vulnerable until suddenly, with an almighty hiss, the screen burst and deflated giving the crew just enough space to jump down.

Now on the beach without a tank, Albert and his crew were wondering what to do next when 'the Germans made our minds up for us'. A machine gun opened up on them, causing them to scatter. As the bullets pinged off the hull of the tank Albert dived round the back to seek some cover.

Pinned down and unable to get a real sense of the battle that was raging around him, he was scared the enemy may start to push the liberating troops back into the sea and approach the tank to finish him off so, after some time, he peered out to see what was happening. His commander, Lieutenant Hawley, and the driver, Trooper Warboys, had been shot as the machine gun sprayed the tank and were lying dead on the beach. He and Hawley had been part of the same tank crew since fighting together in the desert in 1942 and were very close.

The bunker in which Albert has been photographed housed a German 50mm anti-tank gun on D-Day and is immediately beside the place his tank was knocked out.

Seeing Hawley and Warboys dead on the beach is a moment that has etched itself into Albert's memory. Each year on 6 June he returns to that spot to remember and honour his friends killed on D-Day.

77

# Reg Burge

## 2nd Battalion, The Devonshire Regiment

### La Belle Épine

On 13 June Reg was driving a Bren Gun Carrier (a roofless armoured vehicle designed to carry personnel or weapons) that was removing wounded from Tilly-sur-Seulles. He was taking them back to a dressing station in an orchard in La Belle Épine, about seven kilometres away. At the centre of Tilly lay a crossroads, making it strategically important to both the Allies and the Germans. The fighting around the town was extremely fierce and resulted in many casualties on both sides.

After making several trips, and undoubtedly helping save the lives of a significant number of men, Reg returned again to deliver more wounded, but this time he wasn't alone; a German tank had found its way into the orchard, and having seen Reg arrive it immediately turned its gun on him. He had no time whatsoever to react. The tank opened fire and destroyed the Carrier.

Reg has no knowledge of what happened after that. He awoke sometime later in a hospital with severe injuries. He was blind, wheelchair bound and had complete amnesia. It would be a year before he'd regain his eyesight.

He has no idea of how he survived or who saved him from the wreck of the Carrier that day. He can only speculate that as the driver's position was low down and offered a modicum of protection it was probably this that saved his life. Reg has tried hard to find out what happened to the rest of the crew and the wounded he was carrying, sadly to no avail. But he knows that as their positions in the Carrier were more exposed, it is likely he was the only survivor of the attack.

# Len Fox

## RASC, attached to 53rd Welsh Division

### Tilly-sur-Seulles

Len landed on Gold Beach late on D-Day. As a despatch rider his job was to carry messages between units and to escort columns of vehicles to their destinations.

In mid-July he was leading a column of lorries containing ammunition to the front line. Beside the road a sign read 'Dust Kills' – a warning implying dust created by moving vehicles, if spotted, would most certainly bring about enemy fire. But it was a very dry time of year and trying to move a column of lorries around without creating any kind of telltale sign was a near impossibility. As he reached the crossroads behind him in the photograph he stopped to get his bearings. Unbeknownst to Len, the Germans had the crossroads marked as a target for their artillery and they were watching them.

The first shell landed just metres away from them. Len suspected it was a ranging shell and the next one wouldn't miss. They had to move at once.

He got the convoy moving away from the crossroads as quickly as he could but it was too late. Another shell came over and this time hit one of the trucks, setting off all the ammunition it was carrying. The resulting explosion was enormous.

Len was badly wounded. He has no idea how long it was until someone got to him or what happened in the aftermath, as he didn't regain consciousness until he was in a casualty clearing station about ten kilometres back from the crossroads. When he eventually came round he saw a woman all in white and thought he was facing an angel. The nurse he had seen offered him a cigarette and he realised then he wasn't dead because he 'knew you couldn't smoke in heaven!'

Len awoke to find he was temporarily deafened by the blast and he had to have shrapnel removed from his spine.

However, after just six weeks recovery he rejoined his unit to take part in the liberation of Brussels.

# Vera Hay, Légion d'honneur

## QA Nurse. 79th British Military General Hospital

### Le Château de Beaussy, near Bayeux

A few days after the landings the grounds of the Château de Beaussy became a field hospital for British troops. It had a critical role, as major surgeries were often performed there to make a casualty stable enough to survive the trip back to England.

Vera trained as a nurse in Hammersmith Hospital and was one month into a four-year contract when war broke out. She endured the horrors of the Blitz whilst training and had no doubt in her mind that she wanted to help fighting troops as soon as she could. So when she finished her training in August 1943 she volunteered for the Queen Alexandra's Imperial Military Nursing Service and eventually found herself landing on Gold Beach about a week after D-Day. She was one of the first British nurses to land in Normandy.

The sixteen-kilometre journey from the beach to the château took about twenty-four hours to complete, as they had to avoid pockets of German resistance on the way. As a Junior Sister she was part of a team that treated up to 200 casualties per day, prioritising the cases as they arrived, the more serious being rushed straight through to surgery.

It was exhausting work. There was no on/off rotation; everyone was required to work round the clock, sleeping when they had the chance, usually for no more than one or two hours at a time. And when the rare opportunity for rest came, Vera had to find comfort in a ditch until eventually tented accommodation was provided for the sisters.

This photograph was taken on 6 June 2013. It was the first time Vera had been back to the château since the war.

# Fred Lee

## Royal Navy, aboard HMS *Nith*

### Gold Beach

As the invasion fleet crossed the Channel and made its way towards the coast of Normandy on the night of 5/6 June, Fred was on boiler watch aboard HMS *Nith*. Her role was that of Headquarters ship for the landing craft taking the assault forces of 231st Brigade on to Gold Beach. Fred came off watch about 08:00 and remembers hearing shells scream overhead as the ship met opposition from enemy coastal guns. The first sight to greet him on D-Day was that of dead bodies floating past his ship. However the shelling was comparatively light and *Nith* got through the day without incident.

Her next job was to control the routing of the convoys coming in to the beach as part of the build-up phase in the days following D-Day. In the early hours of 24 June Fred was suddenly and unexpectedly put on action stations on the port side – his usual position was on the starboard side. He heard the rattle of the ship's guns engaging a target and moments later the vessel was rocked by a huge explosion. He saw what he thought were sparks but he soon realised they were pieces of lethal hot shrapnel flying through the air.

The ship had been attacked by a Mistel, a deadly new German weapon comprised of two aircraft attached to each other. A pilotless Junkers 88 packed with 7,715 lbs of high explosives was guided by a Me-109 and released on to its target with devastating effect.

They lost power and amid the complete darkness there was talk of abandoning the ship. But fortunately she listed to port, which brought the damage on the starboard side out of the water, removing any immediate danger.

It was a close call for Fred; had he been in his usual place on the starboard side it may well have cost him his life. In total the blast killed nine men and injured a further twenty-five. As daylight came, an American hospital ship arrived alongside the *Nith* and took all her wounded on board. After some temporary patching-up she was towed back to the Isle of Wight for repairs, the crew committing the dead to sea en route.

# Jack Woods

## 9th Battalion, The Royal Tank Regiment

### Hill 112

On 23 March 1942, deciding to take as much charge as he could of the direction of the inevitable military service awaiting him, Jack enlisted in the Royal Armoured Corps. It was his eighteenth birthday.

Six months later, after completing his training, he was posted to 9th Battalion, The Royal Tank Regiment and trained as a Gunner/Mechanic on Churchill tanks. He landed in Normandy on 20 June as part of the follow-up forces and two days later he was told his battalion would take part in Operation Epsom, a massive offensive intended to capture Caen.

Jack was ordered to drive a Humber Scout Car as an injured driver needed replacing. Having never driven one before, he was told to drive the vehicle around a field for a while to get the feel for it. The next time he drove it was into battle the following morning.

After four days of fighting, Epsom failed to achieve its objectives and British troops were withdrawn. Jack's unit were in the process of pulling back when they were counter-attacked by German tanks. He was ordered to leave the Humber as it presented the enemy with an obvious target, so they got out and continued on foot to link up with the infantry. Jack says it was a sign of how 'green and badly trained we were' that they left the car without thinking to take the Bren gun with them.

On 10 July Operation Jupiter commenced. High ground between the rivers Odon and Orne remained in German hands following the failure of Epsom and part of the operation's objectives was to capture it. Known as Hill 112, it offered excellent fields of fire and some of the most commanding views over the entire battle zone. It is reputed one senior German officer stated, 'He who holds Hill 112, holds Normandy'.

The fighting on the hill was some of the most horrific of the whole Normandy campaign. It was in this area that the Germans deployed their most elite forces – eighty-five per cent of all SS units in Normandy with over 1,200 tanks at their disposal were fighting hard for this ground. The British lost 2,000 men in the first two days alone.

Jack served his time on the hill but then luck played its part as he was ordered to accompany a damaged tank back to Brigade Headquarters and remain with it while it was repaired, and so was spared the miserable fate of many of the tank crews embroiled in the battle still raging on the slopes.

It would take a month of combat to dislodge the enemy and finally place the hill in Allied hands.

# James Corrigan

## 6th Battalion, Durham Light Infantry

### Rucqueville

Once the initial assault troops had broken through the coastal defences of Gold Beach on the morning of D-Day, the follow-up battalions started to move inland. James was part of these forces. Their role was to seize objectives further inland before the Germans had a chance to recover.

The 6th Battalion of The Durham Light Infantry had covered good ground and late in the afternoon of 7 June James arrived at a farm belonging to Monsieur and Madame Bedouet, in Rucqueville. The Germans had been in the village but the arrival of the Durhams, along with tanks from the Royal Dragoon Guards, caused them to pull back. After being welcomed by the couple, James and the rest of the soldiers moved into the orchard behind the farm to take up defensive positions.

James hastily dug himself a foxhole - in the exact place he is standing in the photograph - and it wasn't a moment too soon. In response to the Durhams taking up positions around the farm, the enemy started to mortar them. It was a heavy bombardment. As the rounds came down all around him, some bursting in the surrounding trees, lethal pieces of shrapnel and sharp wood splinters rained down on the dug-in troops. James was knocked out after being hit on the head by a large branch that fell from the overhanging tree.

When he came to, the bombardment had stopped. However, there was talk of a possible enemy infantry attack so the troops started to make preparations to defend the area. Just then, a young boy ran out from the farm towards the Durham's positions. It was Bernard, the Bedouet's son. James watched him with great curiosity moving round the orchard and stopping at each foxhole. It wasn't until he approached James that he realised what the boy was doing. Bernard had a bucket of fresh milk and was handing it out to all the troops. Touched by his bravery and good nature, James gave him some sweets in return and with that, Bernard ran back inside the farm.

The Durhams were at the farm for almost three days and were regularly mortared. During that time Bernard made numerous trips to the foxholes with milk and eggs, his visits becoming more and more frequent as his confidence grew.

The little boy who risked his life so many times to bring food to James and his fellow soldiers spent his entire life on the farm. Now in his seventies, Bernard owns the farm where each year on 6 June, James visits him for lunch. He gives him a bottle of whiskey and in return Bernard gives him a bottle of Calvados. Together they raise a glass to James' friends and all the other British soldiers who never returned home from Normandy.

# Victor Mackenzie, Légion d'honneur

## RASC, attached to 7th Armoured Division

### River Orne, Ranville

Victor joined the army in November 1942. He started his time as a driver of a Bren Gun Carrier in the King's Royal Rifle Corps, but his notable driving skills earned him a transfer to the Royal Army Service Corps following his application in 1943.

He landed on Gold Beach on 8 June in an American Mack Truck and was responsible for taking ammunition to tanks and anti-tank guns at the front line.

Towards the end of July he was second in a column of trucks crossing a bridge erected by British engineers over the River Orne in Ranville to take supplies to troops in the airborne sector. As the truck in front of Victor's reached the other side and started to ascend the bank, a German shell landed next to it. The truck took the full force of the explosion and was blown on to its side. Inside were three of Victor's friends who were killed instantly.

A piece of shrapnel from the shell had shot through Victor's windscreen and cut the side of his head. He had no idea he had been wounded. As soon as the shell landed Victor instinctively stopped his truck but was immediately ordered to keep moving by a nearby military policeman.

When he reached his destination, Victor stepped out of the truck and saw that it was peppered with shrapnel holes. It was then that he realised how close he'd come to losing his life. Not only had he now found the cut on the side of his head but also the piece of shrapnel that caused it, lodged in the rifle rack behind where he had been sitting.

Victor kept the piece of shrapnel and still has it today, serving as a reminder of how lucky he was and that not everyone was as fortunate. Each year, when he returns to Normandy for the commemorations, Victor goes to Ranville Cemetery and visits the graves of his three friends who gave their lives that day.

# Wally Fuller

## 144 Regiment, Royal Armoured Corps

### Arromanches

144 Royal Armoured Corps landed on Gold Beach as part of the follow-up armoured support for troops already fighting in Normandy. Wally was a Gunner/Mechanic on a Crusader tank that had been adapted for anti-aircraft purposes. His role was that of main gunner, but he was also trained to drive the tank should the need arise.

After landing on 8 June, he and his crew exited the beach by driving up the ramp behind him in the photograph and started to make their way through the town of Arromanches.

The tank moved along the high street and, as he and another member of the crew were removing the waterproofing from the back of the tank, a man suddenly appeared from a nearby house and ran towards them. Fearing the man may have been carrying an anti-tank grenade Wally instinctively grabbed his rifle.

The man continued to rush towards them but just then Wally spotted what was actually in his hand. He held his fire. As he got to the back of the tank, Wally watched him raise his arm to throw them a bunch of flowers. It was a simple gesture of gratitude from a Frenchman who'd come to celebrate the arrival of the Allies.

# Graham Stevenson

## B Squadron, Nottinghamshire Yeomanry, Sherwood Rangers

### Fontenay-le-Pesnel

Graham missed the DD tank training in the run up to the landings and so was unable to participate in the Sherwood Rangers assault on D-Day. He landed two weeks later to rejoin his squadron and take up his role as Gunner/Radio Operator in a Sherman tank.

On the evening of 11 July his was one of three tanks providing armoured support to an infantry company in a holding position in Fontenay-le-Pesnel. They knew a German attack was imminent.

Graham spotted a six man patrol not far away. At first glance they appeared to be friendly, as one was pushing a British folding bike, but he asked the tank's commander to look and make sure. They turned out to be the leading element of the German attack, so Graham instantly opened fire with the tank's machine gun.

This stirred up a hornet's nest and they immediately came under heavy mortar, tank and machine gun fire. One of the Shermans suffered a direct hit and burst into flames and even though 'mortars were raining down like pennies from heaven', Graham's commander rushed out with a fire extinguisher to help the crew.

After a while Graham opened the hatch of the tank to peer outside, but as he did so a mortar struck the back of his tank and the blast knocked him back in. He was shaken but unhurt.

When things had finally quietened down they found they had become separated from the infantry, who they usually relied on for reconnaissance, so the troop officer decided to go out on foot to recce the area to see if there were still any Germans nearby. Graham offered to accompany him but the moment he stepped down from the tank he was hit in the arm by machine gun fire that came from an enemy tank hidden in a wood.

He was knocked out and awoke a little later to find himself on a jeep bouncing through an orchard, a medic clinging onto him to prevent him from falling off. They made it to a casualty clearing station where Graham was given five pints of blood to stabilise him before eventually being flown back to the UK.

# Related titles published by Helion & Company

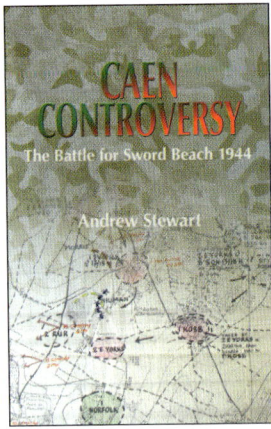

Caen Controversy: the Battle for Sword Beach 1944

Andrew Stewart

ISBN 978-1-909982-12-3 (hardback)

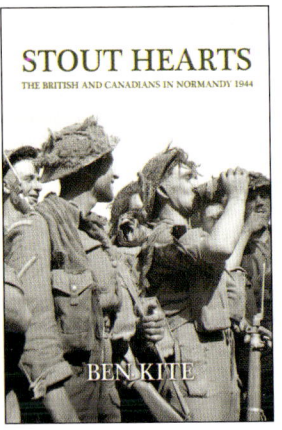

Stout Hearts: The British and Canadians in Normandy 1944

Ben Kite

ISBN 978-1-909982-55-0 (hardback)

Waffen-SS Armour in Normandy. The Combat History of
SS Panzer Regiment 12 and SS Panzer Jagerjäger Abteilung
12, Normandy 1944, based on their original war diaries

Norbert Számvéber

ISBN 978-1-907677-24-3 (hardback)

Mettle and Pasture: the History of the Second Battalion
the Lincolnshire Regiment during World War II

G.J. Weight

ISBN 978-1-909982-14-7 (hardback)

**HELION & COMPANY**

26 Willow Road, Solihull, West Midlands B91 1UE, England

Telephone 0121 705 3393     Fax 0121 711 4075

Website: http://www.helion.co.uk

Twitter: @helionbooks    |    Visit our blog http://blog.helion.co.uk